Text by Elena Pasquali
Illustrations copyright © 2011 Giuliano Ferri
This edition copyright © 2011 Lion Hudson

Published by Lion Children's Books
an imprint of
Lion Hudson plc
Wilkinson House, Jordan Hill Road,
Oxford OX2 8DR, England
www.lionhudson.com/lionchildrens

Paperback ISBN 978 0 7459 6249 8
Hardback ISBN 978 0 7459 6334 1
e-ISBN 978 0 7459 6763 9

First paperback edition 2011
First hardback edition 2012

Acknowledgments
Bible extracts are taken or adapted from the Good News Bible published by the Bible Societies
and HarperCollins Publishers, © American Bible Society 1994, used with permission.

A catalogue record for this book is available
from the British Library

Printed and bound in China, September 2012, LH17

The Animals' Christmas

Elena Pasquali ✦ Illustrated by Giuliano Ferri

LION
CHILDREN'S

Even after everything came true, Mary could never quite believe what had happened.

One day in Nazareth, an angel had spoken to her.

"God has chosen you," the angel said, "to be the mother of his Son, Jesus.

"God will make him a king, such as the world has never seen."

And in spite of the angel's heavenliness, Mary almost giggled. "I'm not even married yet," she said.

"Everything is possible for God," said the angel.

"I know," said Mary, now flustered. "So… yes. I want to do as God wants."

And then the angel was gone, and Mary stood wondering as petals drifted down and a white dove fluttered into the sky.

When Joseph heard that Mary was expecting a baby, he was upset.

"Maybe I shouldn't marry her," he fretted. "I'm not the baby's father."

But that night, when Joseph was sleeping, an angel stepped into his dreams.

"Take Mary as your wife," said the angel. "Take care of her child, too. God will make him a king, such as the world has never seen."

The wedding was agreed; but then came an order from
the Roman emperor that had to be obeyed.
  "Everyone must go to their home town. There they
must put their names on the official list of taxpayers."

"My home town is Bethlehem," said Joseph to Mary.
"Let us go there together. We are going to be family –
you and me, and soon the baby."

So they loaded a donkey, and made their way.

They found the little town crowded. People shrieked with delight as they greeted their relatives. A runaway goat skittered down the street. It startled the donkey and nearly tripped Joseph.

"Do you think there will be anywhere left for us to stay?" asked Mary anxiously.

To their dismay, Mary and Joseph found that
all the rooms were full.

"We can still find a roof to shelter you," declared
one woman determinedly.

She opened the door to a stable and shook a blanket
over the straw.

From the shadows an ox bellowed gently, and a newborn
calf sighed in her sleep.

As she rested in the stable, Mary knew that her baby
would soon be born.

On the hillsides nearby, shepherds huddled around a fire.
  "There have been so many attacks on the sheep this year,"
they grumbled.
  "How close is that wolf we can hear howling?"
  "Do you believe old Reuben, who says he saw a leopard?"

Then all at once, it seemed as if a spark
flew up from the fire and lit the sky.
An angel voice rang out:
  "A fine night, and all is well!
  "In Bethlehem, heaven has come to earth.
  "God's Son is born, and lies in a manger.
  "Don't be afraid, just go and see.
"Glory to God! And peace on earth."

When the sky fell dark again, the shepherds looked uneasily at one another.

"Was that a dream?"

"A trick of the light?"

"Only one way to find out. We'll have to go to Bethlehem."

So they fastened the sheepfold and went, all thoughts of danger banished.

As the shepherds made their way along winding tracks, other men were preparing to ride away from the palace in Jerusalem.

"King Herod is watching us go," whispered one.

"He was not pleased to hear our news – that a new king has been born," agreed another.

"I fear he is dangerous," added a third. "I sensed danger throughout his palace, but at least he has told us where we might find that special king."

As they started off toward Bethlehem, the bright star they had followed for so many days once again shone from the heavens. It was picking out the road as a ribbon of light. Behind them, in the night, a lion roared.

The starlight led the men to the place where Mary and Joseph had taken shelter. As they halted, they exchanged puzzled glances.

"The star was the sign that a king had been born," said one. "Can this really be his birthplace?"

"It is little more than a barn."

"But then, he is to be a king, such as the world has never seen. Come, let us take our gifts."

So they unpacked their gold and frankincense and myrrh and took them inside.

Mary and Joseph, shepherds and wise men: they all believed that the baby born in Bethlehem was a king, such as the world had never seen.

He was the one who would establish a peaceable kingdom, where animals both wild and tame would live together.

"A new king will arise from among David's descendants…
He will rule his people with justice and integrity.

"Wolves and sheep will live together in peace,
and leopards will lie down with young goats.
Calves and lion cubs will feed together,
and little children will take care of them.
Cows and bears will eat together,
and their calves and cubs will lie down in peace.
Lions will eat straw as cattle do.
Even a baby will not be harmed
if it plays near a poisonous snake…
The land will be as full of knowledge of the Lord
as the seas are full of water."

FROM ISAIAH 11